Cover: "A Member of the Poultry Club"
Photography Collection, The New York Public Library
Origin unknown, 1860-1920

Fifty-Two Snapshots: A Memoir Starter Kit
Copyright © Sonja Livingston, 2020

Also by the author:

Ghostbread
Queen of the Fall
Ladies Night at the Dreamland
The Virgin of Prince Street

FIFTY-TWO SNAPSHOTS

A MEMOIR STARTER KIT

"The past is never dead. It's not even past."
                    —William Faulkner

Introduction

Because we've landed together on this page, I'm betting you already understand the power of personal stories to move us. Joan Didion famously wrote, "We tell ourselves stories in order to live." Didion's words may sound a tad dramatic but they're true. Our stories are both precious and necessary. They allow us to make sense of ourselves, each other and the larger world. Sharing our stories is like weaving a rope that connects us to others throughout place and time—which makes writing the closest thing to magic I know. In fact, when it comes to the benefit of getting our stories down on paper, most of us don't need to be convinced.

Instead we struggle with where or how to begin.

So we put the project off for another day, another year, another decade. Or we decide to begin and do what we can to work up to the task. We buy craft books, sign up for workshops and attend readings by authors we admire. We seek out the finest materials—German-engineered pens or handbound journals blessed by Tibetan monks. We attend writing retreats, travel to our ancestors' ranch in New Mexico and buy a turquoise-studded cowboy hat to realign our chakras before we write a word. We seek inspiration from famous writers and try to emulate their routines. Upon discovering that Hemingway wrote standing up and Joan Didion started her day with Coca Cola and a handful of almonds, we do the same—but become exhausted by all the standing and the early morning sugar rush.

On some level, we understand that writing requires only two things: something to write with and something to write on. Still, the task can feel monumental, which makes all the procrastination and preparation understandable and even kind of fun. There's nothing wrong with trying to cultivate your writerly mojo and seeking out the right path. The only problem is that you arrived on the planet loaded with all the mojo you'll ever need and the "right" path is whichever one you take.

Just beneath our fear of beginning often lurks another concern—one that every writer must face. This is the deep-seeded insecurity that we might use our voices but no one will want to hear. You might love reading family stories, for instance, but have a hard time believing that anyone will want to read yours. *My life has not been that interesting*, people say all the time, or they wonder aloud if their stories can possibly be meaningful. The answer is always and forever a resounding yes. Humility is a wonderful and increasingly rare virtue—one that's essential to good memoir writing—but it's misplaced when it undermines the significance of your own story or the need you have to tell it.

In the past two decades, I've led memoir workshops for adult learners, first generation college students, senior citizens, graduate students, high schoolers, church groups, library patrons and community center members. I've visited schools across the country, taught in Mexico, Scotland, Ireland and worked with students in Asia, Canada, Europe and South America while teaching online. In all that time and in all those places, I have yet to meet a person without a worthwhile story. While it's true that on the surface some lives seem more dramatic than others, whether you want to write about the loss of your beloved partner, the years you lived in Brazil, or the daily walks you've taken around the same block for the past fifty years, the stories we tell boil down to a few basic themes. Love and loss. Hope and fear. Desire, discovery and despair. We're all dipping into the same pool of human emotion. It's the way we tell our stories and the specific circumstances of our particular loves and losses that makes them new. Which is why we never tire of reading them.

We crave the connection that comes from well-written memoirs and personal essays. The more we move away from each other— geographically, culturally, spiritually—the more this hunger grows. True stories and memoirs have become incredibly popular over the past few decades, just as our connections to each other are increasingly severed or digitized. Human beings have a basic need to know each other and to be known. It's how we make meaning of the world outside and within. A personal story begins with the particulars of a single life but when it's approached honestly and with care, taps into the overarching human story and becomes a portal through which we explore the experience of being alive.

This series of 52 writing prompts, one per week, is designed to get you writing your own stories, one short "snapshot" at a time. It offers a low-pressure, high-impact way to begin a memoir or longer writing project.

Start with a Snapshot

I wrote my first memoir, GHOSTBREAD, as a series of snapshots. I'd remember something and write it down. I might remember the time someone stole the silver dollar from the coat closet in 1st grade or the time I got ice skates for Christmas when we lived on the Tonawanda Indian Reservation near Buffalo. I didn't have a plan for what I was writing necessarily. Memories would simply arrive and I'd do my best to describe them, one snapshot at a time. By snapshot, I don't mean an actual photograph, but a picture, scene, image (a certain sound, taste, scent, touch or sight) that conveys the basic essence and imagery of a memory as it arises.

You may be a very organized sort of person and want to write your stories in perfect detail from birth to present day. There's nothing wrong with that approach. If writing that way works for you, go for it. The problem is that such order doesn't tend to work, or when it does, it produces less dynamic writing, because memory is not an orderly affair. Memory works associatively and symbolically and can seem chaotic and random. But what you remember matters. Your memory is not perfect in the way of a transcript. Instead, it's perfect in the way of wisdom and discovery. This booklet is intended to help you make memory your friend and partner in crime instead of trying to force it into a predetermined form. The idea is to pay attention to the memories that come as a result of the prompts (and outside of them) and to follow where they lead.

This booklet is made up of exercises I've relied on over the years as both a teacher and a writer. I've included some old photographs from friends and a few quotes about writing. This handful of words and smattering of images are more than enough to guide you. You can and should study craft by reading what inspires, informs and delights you, by paying attention to how sentences are put together and by exploring the endless possibilities of language. In time, to make your stories come more alive for readers you will need to revise, expand and intensify the elements of good writing—such as specific details, precise language, sensory images, and dialogue—but let's save that for another day. Today is about getting the words on the page.

Prompts & Lists
Nothing helps writers face the blank page as much as a prompt. By prompt, I mean a writing exercise that asks you to explore a particular subject or some facet of experience, often in very a particular way. The prompt might ask you to write about your favorite childhood pet, for instance. It's as simple as that but works because it focuses your racing mind, narrows your scope and provides a specific point from which the writing can

naturally blossom and grow. The prompt simply provides a place to begin. I've found that it almost does not matter *where* you start but *that* you start. The stories inside you are like underground streams just waiting for any opening that allows them to emerge. Prompts are like divining rods or tiny drills that locate and tap into what's already alive and moving beneath the surface.

I've included enough prompts in this booklet for you to respond weekly for the next year. If you decide to write once a week, you might start on a specific day with a new prompt, then use 10 minutes per day of the following week to expand and refine that first draft. If you don't have time for daily practice, write weekly. If you do have time, feel free respond to the prompts more frequently. The main thing is to write regularly. If you finish the prompt and need more, go back through again. Some offer more than one option. Most can be repeated and will bear different fruit each time. I've also included a few bonus prompts in the end. Which means this little booklet can keep you going for longer than 52 snapshots.

Some prompts will work better than others for the story you're trying to tell. You can proceed in order, or open the book at random and pop around. When a prompt is challenging, be patient and give it your best effort—but there's no need to force it. If it doesn't work, write about why it doesn't work or turn it on its head, writing the opposite of what's been prescribed. If you don't want to write about your favorite pet, write about an animal you could not stand or the problem with pets or what it's like to have cat allergies. There is no wrong way to respond to a prompt. Anything that gets your pen moving is a win.

Many of the prompts involve making lists. This may seem very much like not writing at first. But lists provide a wonderful way to begin. Everyone knows how to make a list. You already do it for grocery shopping and planning your day. Lists result in a bunch of quickfire images which are often powerful in their own right, but which also serve as a storehouse of ideas to return to. In this way, one prompt can lead to several snapshots. One of the first prompts asks you to list some of your early memories. It doesn't ask you to remember them in chronological order or to decide what they all mean. All that comes later. For now, you only need to slow down, pay attention to what arises and let your pen fly.

Bells & Whistles

I'm endlessly astonished by what writers can do with a few minutes. I'm also frequently blown away by just how stunning what we remember can be. Give yourself a set amount of time for each prompt. I recommend 15-20 minutes, but more or less is okay. Even 5 minutes will get you somewhere. No matter how many minutes you decide on, stick with it and show up according to whatever schedule you've devised.

It's essential to decide where and when you will write. Inspiration is a nice but if you don't plan and prioritize your writing time, it is far less likely to happen. Many writers schedule their writing time as a regular appointment. This may not seem very Romantic but it is effective. Books are written a few minutes and few sentences at a time. What a relief! You don't have to figure it all out in one sitting, you simply need to write something today. One snapshot this week. Another next week. And so on. You don't need to know where it all leads. So ease up and try to enjoy this low-pressure and spontaneous way into your material.

This little booklet is about making full use of the mysterious awkward challenging shimmering moments that make up our lives. The difference between the would-be memoirist and the actual memoirist lies in what you do with these moments. So go ahead: Grab your pen or open your laptop and choose a prompt. Or look at that old photograph of your mother posing on the Jersey Shore back in 1928 and write about what you see. You don't need any fancy formulas, writerly secrets or pull-out charts. You don't need any bells and whistles. You are the bell. You are the whistle. You have everything you need to begin right now.

"I can begin anywhere. With anything. Turn it in any direction. It's all dipping into the same pot. But a pot of my shaping, my hands on the clay."
—Judith Kitchen

The Sweetest Sound

They say your name is the sweetest sound. What's the story of your name? How and why was it given to you? You can include research about the name's meaning or write about nicknames, childhood taunts or pronunciation troubles. You might write about a name you chose for yourself—a Confirmation or hyphenated last name. If you prefer, write about someone else's name. Explore a name that mystifies or intrigues you. Compile a list of family names. There's no wrong way to respond to this prompt.

I Remember

Part 1: Write the words "I Remember" at the top of a page. Next—without overthinking it—make a list of memories. Write whatever comes to mind. Be specific. Instead of writing, "I remember the first day of my new school," say something about it, like the way the classroom looked as big as a football field or the other kids stared or you looked at the ground for an entire hour. Challenge yourself to conjure memories that engage not only sight, but sound, scent, taste, and touch. For example, if you remember the day your dog ran away, describe the color of his fur and how fluffy it was. If you remember your grandma's unique scent, tell us it was like mint and Vaseline and the lavender candies she always chewed. Such sensory details will bring your memories to life for readers. Grab your pen or laptop and make a list of whatever comes. Write for 5 minutes.

Part 2: Choose one of these memories to expand into a paragraph or two. Keep this list to return to. Expand another memory when you get stuck.

Option #2:   Make a list of what you don't remember, or what you wish you remember, etc..

Beneath the Surface

What can't people tell by looking at you? What things do others not see? What do people assume about you and get wrong? Make a list. Choose one and flesh it out.

Playlist

A friend recently described her final radiation treatment. "Can't Help Falling in Love," by Elvis Presley came on the radio while she waited. This was her mother's favorite song and hearing it allowed her to just sit there and cry in the waiting room.

Music can move us in powerful ways.

Yesterday, I had Tanya Tucker's "Delta Dawn," stuck in my head and couldn't shake it loose. Any song by Michael Jackson or Madonna will take me back to high school. Make a list of songs that connect you to other times, people and places. Write about one.

Cher, Beyonce & Mr. Clean

When I was about 6, I liked to imagine that Cher was my mother. She looked so exotic and beautiful on her album cover. The essayist Dinty W. Moore has written about imagining the powerful and effective Mr. Clean as his father. Sue William Silverman wrote an entire book about her devotion to the all-American Pat Boone. Each of these figures represented something we were missing as kids.

What famous (or larger-than-life) person did you dream about—either as a parental figure, best friend or crush? Did you pretend Beyonce might be your prom date? Did the man in the local Beatles cover band with the gentle smile become a stand-in for your father even though you never spoke? Was Buffy the Vampire Slayer your sister? Nancy Drew your alter ego? Don't explain why you idolized these strangers, fictional characters or superstars. Instead, snap a Polaroid of the past and show us.

Kung-Fu Lunchbox

Growing up, my worst fear was that people from school would discover my family's poverty. In retrospect, it's pretty clear that our poverty was impossible to hide. But my fear is partly why I hated the Kung-Fu lunchbox I was forced to use in elementary school. The dented metal hand-me-down was the bane of my existence for the better part of a year.

Many of us felt we had to hide something as children. It might have been something about ourselves, a family member, our neighborhood or our home. What did you hope no one would see when you were a kid? Is there an object associated with this? Take this prompt in two parts:
1. Make a list what you hoped no one would see.
2. Choose one and describe an object that represented that particular shame or fear and write about it.

Stepping Stones

Imagine your life up to this point as a path. What are the most important moments/events/decisions that led you to where you are today? Write down the top ten. If considering your entire life is too wide a timeframe, break it down by decades or some other more manageable chunks of time.

Choose one stepping stone to expand today. Next time you return to this page, expand another. And so on.

Present Tense and Common Sense

Writing is about noticing. Even memoir, which is about the past, is really about paying close attention and trying to remember what was playing on the radio, to channel the scent of baking bread or the feel of old carpet under your bare feet—these sensory details are exactly what make writing come to life for readers.

To practice this essential writing skill, choose a memory—maybe your very first memory—and write about it in present tense, as if you are there now. Instead of writing: *I was sitting on the porch looking at the men fishing*; write: *I am sitting on the porch, listening to the crows caw as the men stand silent and unmoving with fishing poles in their hands.*

Writing in present tense may feel strange at first (and it can always be changed back after you finish writing) but it can help tune us into the sights/sounds/textures/tastes/scents of memory in ways that past tense can miss.

Time Travel

One of my favorite book titles is, I HAVE TO GO BACK TO 1994 AND KILL A GIRL, by Karina McGlynn. The title of her poetry book speaks to the way that imagination allow us to travel into the past. Moving around in time and revisiting moments with the awareness you lacked then can be a surprisingly powerful approach in memoir. This prompt has two parts.

1.) Make a list of moments you'd like to return to. They might even be moments you weren't present for.

2.) Choose one and flesh it out. As in the previous prompt, try present tense.

Optional: Borrow McGlynn's formula and title your piece "I have to go back to _____ and_____," such as "I have to go back to Omaha and find a man named Al," or "I have to go back to 1968 and stop my mother's first date." If you describe a moment you didn't inhabit, give yourself permission to imagine that scene while staying true to the reality of what you know about the people involved and facts.

"A good snapshot stops a moment from running away."
—Eudora Welty

Time Travel, Part II

We've all had interactions in which we didn't say exactly what we wanted to say. Only afterwards were we much clearer about what we wish we would have said. Make a list of such moments then choose one that resonates. Return to a time when you did not say what was in your head or your heart, possibly a time when you were silent or constrained by the setting or fear. Go back, set the scene and write what you wish you would have said.

Mea Culpa

In 2nd grade, I helped my classmates put a tack in another girl's chair. The next year, I stole a Chunky candy bar from the store (and was shocked and disappointed to learn it was loaded with raisins). Another time, I stole a boy's idea to use Snoopy and his sidekick, Woodstock, for an "Officer Friendly" poster assignment and never gave the boy credit, even when my poster won the schoolwide award.

What do you still feel guilty about? Make a list. Choose one and write about it. Come back later and write another. Guilt may not feel very good, but, like its cousin shame, it can preserve a moment's intensity like nothing else.

This I (Used To) Believe

Think back to a time when you had a clear view on an important issue or idea. Perhaps you believed that marriage should last forever, that lying is inevitable, that babies are delivered by storks. Whatever it was, write about something you used to believe with your whole heart. Tell what happened to make it change.

Another option: Write what you still believe in.

Why Me?

There are times when it really seems like the world has it in for us. Think back to a time when you asked yourself "Why me?" as a kid, an occasion or event that made it seem like the world was incredibly unfair. Instead of merely explaining what happened, describe the scene with enough detail and imagery to help take readers there with you. It might help to begin this snapshot in with the words: *Why me?*

Excuses

This exercise is modeled on the flash story by Antonia Clark called "Excuses I Have Already Used," in which the writer simply offers a cascade of sometimes funny but increasingly serious excuses—from missing homework to explaining romantic missteps and not showing up for those who really needed her. Your list need not escalate. It might be funny or dramatic or clever or maybe a bit of each. Begin by remembering times you used excuses as a kid, then extend your list to include excuses you used later in life and even now. The list may work perfectly on its own or you can choose one excuse and flesh the story out.

Band Kid, Swimmer, Buffalo Bills Fan

How did you define or differentiate yourself as a kid?
Many of us used our interests, ethnicity, team affiliation
or regionality to show the world who we were. Did you
wear a New Orleans Saints jersey every day for a year?
Were you a band kid? The star skier? The one who
burned smudge sticks in her locker at recess? Write
about an identity you cultivated. Describe what you
wore or said and did. Show us who you were. Take us
there.

Things That Make Your Heart Beat Fast

Sei Shōnagon was a 10ᵗʰ century Japanese courtier who recorded her thoughts, observations and opinions in her PILLOW BOOK. Her mini essays often take the shape of snapshots, poems and lists, such as her "Things that make your heart beat fast," in which she includes: *a sparrow with nestlings, a sudden gust of rain, lighting fine incense, and looking into a clouded Chinese mirror.*

Make your own list of things that made your heart beat fast. If you prefer to use less poetic language, make a list of joys or delights. Spend 5 minutes on your list, choose one item and flesh it out. Or, if you prefer, keep on going with the list and see how it works on its own. Try this from the perspective of a younger version of yourself, then from your present point of view.

PE Class, Sleepovers & Cross-Country Road-Trips

We're all survivors of something. It might be the heart-wrenching loss of a loved one or a cancer diagnosis or something smaller, like waiting in line for concert tickets in the cold or surviving the concert itself. What have you survived? Make a list. The tone can be funny or serious. It's often powerful to include a range of incidents such as:

I survived PE class, Melissa Germano's 6th grade sleepover, my first marriage, a cross-country road trip with my sister, Stage 3 breast cancer, my first Yoga Class, wedding planning at age 75.

Once you make your list, choose one. Swell it into a scene we can practically see and hear and touch.

Medusa, Shark Teeth & Gettysburg

The previous prompt asked about how you styled yourself in the past and the ways you presented yourself to the world. This prompt is about what you really loved, which may or may not be the same thing. For instance, I loved Greek mythology and was especially enchanted by Medusa, but this was not a subject I shared with my friends. Some people are fascinated by tornadoes, Civil War or fossilized shark teeth.

Option 1: Think about the objects and information you amassed as a child and make a list of your obsessions, interests and hobbies. Choose one to expand. Later make a list of what fascinates you now and explore the connections between the lists.

Option 2: What career or future did you imagine for yourself based on your interests? What did others suggest or expect? Why? What did you not allow yourself to imagine? Why not?

Secret of the Old Clock

What did you hold onto as a kid? What did you save—
no matter how often you moved or your mother cleaned
out your room? Maybe you held on to the one Nancy
Drew book you owned, to Vicky Clarkson's denim
Gaucho pants or whatever heartbreaking thing your
sister said to you in the back of the car the day your
mother died.

What do you hold onto now? The tiny virgin Mary stuck
to postage-stamp bock of marble given to you by a
charming monk? The dainty Japanese earrings from a
friend? The primitive milk blue vase your mother made?

Describe what you hung (or hang) onto, its origins and
where it's kept. Let your description reveal its
significance.

What You Saw

What did you once see that you cannot unsee? Where were you? What happened right before? After? Conjure the moment. Make use of details and sensory descriptions to let us see it with you.

My People

Who are your people? Your ancestors, family, or some
other collection of people you know well? They might
be euchre players, Buffalo Bills fans, fellow sugar
addicts, Star Trek convention attendees or Southern
Baptists. There's power in writing about the self as part
of a collective. Think about the various groups to which
you belong and the traits they share. Choose one group
and describe it. Be as funny or serious as you like.

My Mother, Queen of Electricity

My mother used to tell the story of her father running a proselytizing priest out of their house back in Twin Mountain, NH. She also made sure everyone knew that she carried her babies longer than most, staying pregnant for a full ten months instead of the ordinary nine. My mother also claimed to stop any watch she wore on account of all the electricity coursing through her veins. Were these stories true? Maybe. Mostly. It didn't matter. They were hers.

What stories did your parents or family repeat so often they became legends and individual lore?

Misfits, Rebels & Stand-Outs

Who at school or in your neighborhood didn't quite fit in? The woman who wore an elegant fur coat and untied combat boots while digging through garbage cans downtown? The uncle who never married and mumbled to himself from morning to night. The evangelical kids who gathered by the flag pole to pray every morning at East High?

Because belonging is so essential to our survival and not fitting in can feel hazardous as a kid, we often studied those on the periphery—fearful or intrigued by their differences. For this prompt, describe someone who didn't fit in.

Beggars' Night

A handful of kids in my neighborhood put on their costumes the night before Halloween and went out trick-or-treating. This was called Beggars' Night and the rest of us mocked or pitied those unfortunate children whose parents found the actual Halloween too scary to let their kids participate. Today's prompt is inspired by Beggars' Night and has two options:

Option 1:   Write about a time you begged, refused to beg or when someone begged you.

Option 2:   Write about a time a parent or caretaker refused to let you participate with the other kids.

The Body

Write about the body. Yours or another's.

Write about a particular trait or struggle, what you loved or didn't love.

Be as creative or straightforward as you like in your descriptions. Write about your father's hands, your grandmother's eyes or the various home haircuts you suffered. Write about your mother putting on makeup, your sister's café au lait birthmark, or your own gapped teeth or slightly webbed right toe. Write about this as a past struggle or joy or from the perspective of the present day.

Fear

Centipedes. Public speaking. Curtainless windows at night. These are just a few of the things that terrified me as a kid. Make a list of your fears. Be specific. Choose one and expand it.

The Great Beyond

Write about an early experience of death.

Comfort Food

Mac & Cheese. Biscuits and Gravy. Fried Dough. Nana's Coconut Crème Pie.

Food is a natural extension of our people and our places. In fact, you may have already included food in some of your snapshots. This prompt puts food center stage. Write about a food you grew up with, a dish someone made for you, a treat or meal you could count on.

If comfort food doesn't strike a chord, turn it around and write about a food you dreaded.

Food, Part II

The previous prompt asked you to consider a food that was (or is) important to you. This prompt asks you to write about a specialty food important to your entire family, region or culture. Maybe you don't make it like grandpa did, but you do know the secret to a good red sauce or perhaps you've found yourself defending fruitcake, liverwurst or French-Canadian poutine.

Be creative with this snapshot. You might write it as a how-to guide (*How to Make Cuban Black Beans*), a recipe with a memory attached (*Aunt Lola's Pralines with a Memory of Biloxi*), or as an expose or rant about what people get wrong about a food that's important to you (*What They Don't Tell You About Cornbread*).

Inheritance

Option 1:   Write about something handed down.
This might be physical—an object, trait or a feature of
personality, such as a tendency or a habit.

Option 2:   Turn it around and write about what you
did not inherit.

Option 3:   Look in the mirror. Who looks back?
What traces of the past do you carry in your face? Look
again. Without judgment. Write what you see.

"We look at the world once, in childhood.
The rest is memory."

—Louise Gluck

Lost & Found

Part 1:   Describe something you lost and could never get back. Make a list first, if it helps. Choose one and write a paragraph.

Part 2:   Describe something you once found. Write a paragraph.

Part 3:   Connect the above items into one snapshot or choose one to further expand.

BB Gun, Skateboard, Feathered Hair

Write about something you wanted as a kid but did not get. Or maybe you did get it, but getting it did not turn out the way you expected. This might be an object—such as the skateboard or BB gun you longed for on your 9th birthday. It might also be something you generally aspired to— such as a skinny waist, the ability to feather your hair like Farrah Fawcett or to become best friends with Cara Palumbo from 7th period English class. Make a list. Choose one. Describe the object in a way that reveals your longing.

Sicily, 1922

Grab an old photograph. Maybe it's your mother on the farm as a child or an image of Palermo, 1992, from your grandfather's trunk. Who are the people standing outside the small church? Who is the boy waving to the men in the fishing boat and why? What about the girl shading her eyes with a hand? Find a photograph of an ancestor you did not know, a snapshot of your parents as a young couple or an image from your own life.

Even if you know the photograph's subject, study the image and try to go beyond the frame's edges with the power of imagination. What does their expression suggest? Their clothes and the backdrop? What might they have been doing right before the photo was snapped? What were they feeling? What would their days have been like? What do you most wish you could know?

Decoration Day

In parts of Appalachia, families and communities gather on certain Sundays to put flowers on the graves of loved ones and tend the cemeteries. These events involved picnics and singing. What did you celebrate in your neck of the woods? Were there polka festivals? Processions? Quinceañeras? What local produce was celebrated. Ramps? Lilacs? Sweet Potatoes? What are the customs? What food or music is involved? Write about a local tradition and a particular memory of it.

Lunch Ladies, Tater Tots, Middle School Warfare

Write about the school cafeteria. If you didn't eat in a cafeteria, write about the school bus, the playground or some other location where kids were thrown together with minimal supervision. What took place when the adults weren't looking? Where did you sit? Who was nearby? Who was far away? Choose a memory. Show us who you were and what you saw there and then.

Where You Come From

Where we're from is important to our stories but it's easy to overlook or to assume that others will find boring or unrelatable. In fact, the opposite is true. Readers crave setting details. Fortunately, the ways to talk about place are endless.

Write a few paragraphs about where you come from. Focus on your city/town, region or neighborhood. Write about your dead-end street, your mid-sized city or what it means to come from a flyover state. Show us the part of the world that you understand.

Ten Miles South of Lonesome Creek

Just as with people, the names of places are important. They add texture and concrete points of connection to your writing. They can also evoke tone/mood and invite symbolic association.

Part I: Make a list of places you have lived. Be specific. Include the addresses or city/county names. Some of mine are: Leighton Avenue, 78 Grand Avenue, Bowman Street, Orleans County, Thruway Motel in Batavia, Basom Road, 10 Lamont Place.

Part II: List natural features near these places. Bergen Swamp. Lake Ontario. The Great Ridge. Susquehanna Landfill. The Salt River. High Falls. The Forked Deer River. Superstition Mountains.

Part III. Choose a specific place and write about it.

Hint: Save this list and pepper your other pieces with these details when they make sense.

"All you have to do is write one true sentence.
Write the truest sentence that you know."

—Ernest Hemingway

Tiger Lilies, Snake Doctors, Kudzu

Make a list of flora, fauna and natural objects from your region of the world. If southern magnolias and pecan trees grew in your neighborhood, write them down. If you had a lilac or a bunch of peonies with ants on the buds in your front yard, add them to your list. Include the kinds of critters and fish and bugs you'd interact with. If you don't know the name of the tree or flower that grew out back, look it up. Even if you don't think it's important, I promise you it is. After you've written a list, see which one resonates and write a few paragraphs.

Just as with your list of place names, keep this list handy and include some in your other snapshots, even when they are about other things.

Like the Back of Your Hand

The last few prompts have had you write about the places you lived and some natural features of the landscape. Now zoom in. Think of more intimate spaces. Write about the place you know best, a place you feel safe, or return to often in dreams.

For me, it's Corpus Christi Church in Rochester, New York. Yours may be a bedroom in New Jersey, a bar near the railroad tracks in Memphis, the thickest branch of a sugar maple near Niagara Falls, or a particularly welcoming rock along the James River in Richmond.

Take us to this place. Show readers what you see, hear, smell, taste and feel when you are (or were) there.

Long Way Home

Write about a time when you were far from home.

Reverse Role Model

Who or what did you fear becoming? Were you warned against becoming like this person or did you discover this on your own? Either way, describe the person you never wanted to be. Instead of explaining why you didn't want to emulate this person, let the way you describe them speak for itself. Instead of writing: *I never wanted to be my grandmother because she was an alcoholic.* Instead, try revealing that trait through your description of that person: *Anna Mae Chapman loved three things more than anything else: A rare steak, a warm bar stool, and a man who would pick up the tab.*

Letter to the One Who Wronged You

Write a letter to someone who hurt you. Describe what they did. This can be a letter to the woman who cheated and broke your heart, or the boy who swiped your Batman pencil case in 3rd grade. Nothing is too minor. In fact, smaller hurts and minor examples are often easier to write about. Even when dealing with larger hurts, zooming in on a smaller tangible object often conveys emotion more powerfully.

Hosanna. Alleluia. Shalom.

Write a memory of church, temple or a religious space.
If you did not attend religious services, write about the
thing in your life that came closest to church.

Reunions, Weddings & Funerals

Write about a time you gathered with extended family. This might have been a wedding, funeral, reunion, holiday or picnic. What marked the event? Who organized it? What did the bride or groom wear? Was there a dollar dance? A preacher? Music? Incense? What did the women do versus the men? If your family had no gatherings, write about what you did instead.

"There is no greater agony than bearing an untold story inside you."
—Maya Angelou

The Hardest Thing

What did people never say aloud in your family? What were the unspoken rules? What secrets did you keep? Where do you still stumble and look away? What truth still hammers at you but you fear giving it life on the page?

Not every hard thing needs to be written about but some of the things we don't speak have tremendous power. Trust your gut on which hard things to pursue. These will often seem like minor incidents to others but, for you, are surrounded by shame, guilt or fear. Choose just one and write a sentence about it. Just one true sentence, like Hemingway advised. Explore a bit more when you're ready. For today, just open the door.

Failure

The word 'failure' doesn't sound like anything we want to focus on but our losses carry a great deal of weight and offer unique wisdom and insight when we're able to look back at them with generosity and a wider perspective. Write about a time you failed. Maybe it was a road test, making a special dinner, applying to college, or asking someone out.

If you want a happier prompt, turn it around and write about a time you succeeded. But after that, come back and write about failure.

Step on a Crack

Option 1:   What superstitions did you grow up with? Did you avoid stepping on cracks, killing spiders, walking under ladders, or shattering mirrors? Make a list and expand one.

Option 2.   What basic proclamations, unsought advice or warnings did you hear as a child? Were you told to finish your supper and be glad you're not starving; avoid eating too much bread; try to save a dollar a week; know that any job worth doing is worth doing well; stop frowning or your face would freeze that way. Make a list of what you were told. Choose one and expand.

Mystery Date

What games did you play as a kid? Who were your
companions? Did you play hopscotch? Listen to the
Grease soundtrack while dancing in the living room?
Play hide-and-seek with the neighbors, gin rummy with
your uncle, and "Mystery Date" with friends.

Make two columns. In the first, list who you played
with as a kid. Next, list the sorts of things you did. After
you have a good list on both sides, choose a
combination of who and what and how you played and
write a few paragraphs.

The Great Divide(s)

When did you first understand something about race? What did you notice about yourself or others? Who said what? What was never stated but loomed large? Without judgment or excuses, write that memory.

Next time you open to this page, answer the same questions about gender, class, religion or whatever other barrier existed between you and others.

Headlines

What were the big events of your childhood? Elections? Political disasters? Natural disasters? Crimes? Inventions and new technology? For example, the collapse of the Soviet Union, the Atlanta child murders, Diana & Charles' Royal Wedding, the development of microwave ovens and personal computers, and a local serial killer known as the "Alphabet Murderer," were important backdrops to my own understanding of the world.

An awareness of what was happening in the larger world will tie your own life to history and the larger culture in direct and symbolic ways. Think back to what people were talking about when you were young and what you remember as big news. Make a list of local and national items. After you complete your list, choose one that resonates and write it out.

Color Wheel

Choose a color. Any color. Once you've chosen it (don't overthink it!), make a list of things that color from the past. Be specific. Blue is the color of my mother's eyes. Yellow is the peeling paint of the house where the man who sang opera every night lived. Green is the catalpa leaves shaped like hearts in the park where I had solo picnics in college. Writers have filled entire books by simply choosing a color to help tap into and organize images and memories that matter most.

Recap:
1. Choose a color.
2. Make a list of objects, places or features associated with that color.
3. Choose one and expand.
4. When you're stuck, return to this page and spin the color wheel again.

The White Lady of Durand Eastman Park

Rochester, New York's most famous ghost wore a long white dress and roamed Durand Eastman Park at night searching for her lost daughter. Some reported seeing her with her ghostly German Shepherd companions while others heard the sound of weeping. Either way, she was called "The White Lady," and I still can't go up to the lakeshore at night without thinking of her.

Our city also boasted the very real legacy of George Eastman, who started Kodak and later committed suicide. It was home to Susan B. Anthony, Frederick Douglass and the spooky Fox Sisters. Who were your town's famous residents, ghosts and legends? What stories did you hear?

Choose one from your hometown or current city and write it down.

Last Shots (A Handful of Bonus Prompts)

Beautiful, Brave, Bully

We often use abstract labels without considering what they actually convey to others. Think of someone you knew who was brave or beautiful or a bully. Describe them. Don't use the word 'beautiful' or 'bully' in your snapshot. Instead reveal their character through actions, imagery and words.

Gail Mott's Version of Heaven

My mother-in-law thinks Paradise is a place where you find answers to every question. Pretend you've entered Gail's version of heaven. Make a list of what you've always wanted to know. Why is the sky blue? Where do cedar waxwings sleep at night? Why did your father leave? Questions are rocket fuel for writing. Choose one from your list to explore.

Sugar Yourself

Write a letter to the person you once were. Give advice. Don't hold back. Be specific. Use any tone you like. A great example of this comes from the *Dear Sugar* column written by Cheryl Strayed and published on *The Rumpus* (see Source List).

Review a Person, a Relationship, a Year

It's not often effective to harshly judge others in memoir. It's better to describe things as evenly as possible and let readers decide what it all means. This prompt invites you to break the rules and judge up a storm! Review someone like you would on Amazon. You can even assign stars (speaking of which, feel free to review this little booklet!) Rate a particular year, a job, a relationship, a person. Your snapshots will be most powerful when you use concrete descriptions and examples to back up your reviews and claims.

Acknowledgements

Many thanks to my students who've helped me test and refine these prompts. Thanks to Jim Mott for editing and support. Thank you, dear reader, for the bravery to write the necessary and beautiful stories that only you can tell.

Image Credits (used with permission as follows):

- p. 5. "Virginia deBruin, Jersey Shore," c.1928. Permission of Cathy Chin.
- p.17. "Who Are You Looking For?/¿Qué Buscas?" El Paso, Tx/ Ciudad Juárez, Mexico Borderplex, c.1969. Permission of Yasmín Ramírez.
- p. 27. "Purim," Alice de Boton, 1920. Permission of Rachel Hall.
- p. 33. "Swim Team with Uncle Bob (Victor Edward Bouldin)," Jacob Riis High, Los Angeles, CA, 1948-1949. Permission of Aurora M. Lewis.
- p. 39. "What's So Funny?" Cincinnatus NY, c.1943 Permission of Joy Underhill.
- p. 43.   "Big and Little Nancy," Queens, NY, 1960. Permission of Nancy E. McCarthy
- p. 49. "Effie Jeanne Watkins, Age 11," Meridian, MS, 1939. Permission of Susan Cushman.
- p. 57. "Warren Skye, Basom, NY c. 2010. Family photograph.
- p. 65.   "Ferdinando LoBue Family," Rochester, NY c. 1924. Permission of Marie E. Gibson.
- 69. "Cousin Erling," Tucson, AZ, c. 1965. Permission of Lisa Shillingburg.
- p. 75. "Last Shot," Rochester, NY, c. 1970. Permission of Stephanie Livingston Heywood.

Quote Sources (in order of appearance)

- Joan Didion, THE WHITE ALBUM, Simon & Schuster, New York, 1979.
- William Faulkner, REQUIEM FOR A NUN, Random House, New York, 1951.
- Judith Kitchen, generally attributed/DISTANCE AND DIRECTION, Coffee House Press, Minneapolis, 2001.
- Eudora Welty, generally attributed and ONE WRITERS BEGINNINGS, Harvard University Press, Cambridge, MA, 1998.
- Louise Gluck, MEADOWLANDS, Ecco, New York, 1997.
- Ernest Hemingway, A MOVEABLE FEAST, Scribner's, New York, 1964.
- Maya Angelou, I KNOW WHY THE CAGED BIRD SINGS, Random House, New York, 1969.

Resources

- *Brevity* Website: *https://brevitymag.com*.
- *The Rumpus*, Dear Sugar, Col. 64, Feb. 10, 2011. https://therumpus.net

Anthologies of Short Nonfiction

BEST OF BREVITY, Ed. Moore & Bossiere, 2020 IN SHORT, Ed. by Kitchen, 1996 / IN BRIEF, Ed. by Paumier Jones & Kitchen, 1999 / SHORT TAKES, Ed. by Kitchen, 2005 / BRIEF ENCOUNTERS , Ed. Kitchen & Lenney, 2015

A Few Memoirs Written in Snapshots

SAFEKEEPING, Abigail Thomas, 2001 / ANOTHER BULLSHIT NIGHT IN SUCK CITY, Flynn, 2005 / FAMILY OF STRANGERS, Deborah Tall, 2006 / GHOSTBREAD, Sonja Livingston, 2009 BLUETS, Maggie Nelson, 2009 / BOOK OF DELIGHTS, Ross Gay, 2019 / LATE MIGRATIONS, Margaret Renkl, 2019

Made in United States
Troutdale, OR
10/26/2023

14038349R00051